A Pocketful of Stars

For Jamie, with love. Thank you to Jeff, my family,
my friends and the poetry library — N. S-S.
For Nyssa, Amber, Asher and Topaz, with love — E. S-S.

Barefoot Poetry Collections
an imprint of
Barefoot Books
37 West 17th Street
4th Floor East
New York, New York
10010

Introduction copyright © 1999 by Nikki Siegen-Smith
Illustrations copyright © 1999 by Emma Shaw-Smith
The moral right of Emma Shaw-Smith to be identified as the illustrator of this work has been asserted

This book is printed on 100% acid-free paper
Illustrations prepared in watercolor and mixed media on heavyweight paper

Graphic design by Amesbury Grzelinski Ltd, England
Typeset in Bernhard Modern and Heatwave
Color separation by Grafiscan, Verona
Printed and bound in Singapore by Tien Wah Press (Pte) Ltd

1 3 5 7 9 8 6 4 2

Publisher Cataloging-in-Publication Data

A pocketful of stars : poems about the night / compiled by
Nikki Siegen-Smith ; illustrated by Emma Shaw-Smith.—1st ed.
[40]p. : col. ill. ;   cm.
Summary: A magical anthology of poems about the night,
gathered from many countries and cultures. Celebrates the
mysteries of the darkness, as well as the coziness of being tucked
in bed. Poets include Robert Louis Stevenson, Walter de la Mare,
Arnold Adoff and Grace Nichols.
ISBN 1-902283-84-8
1.Night -- Juvenile poetry. 2. Children's poetry. I. Siegen-Smith, Nikki.
II. Shaw-Smith, Emma, ill. III. Title.
808.819--dc21 1999 AC   CIP

A Pocketful of Stars

Poems About The Night

compiled by Nikki Siegen-Smith

illustrated by Emma Shaw-Smith

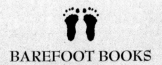

BAREFOOT BOOKS

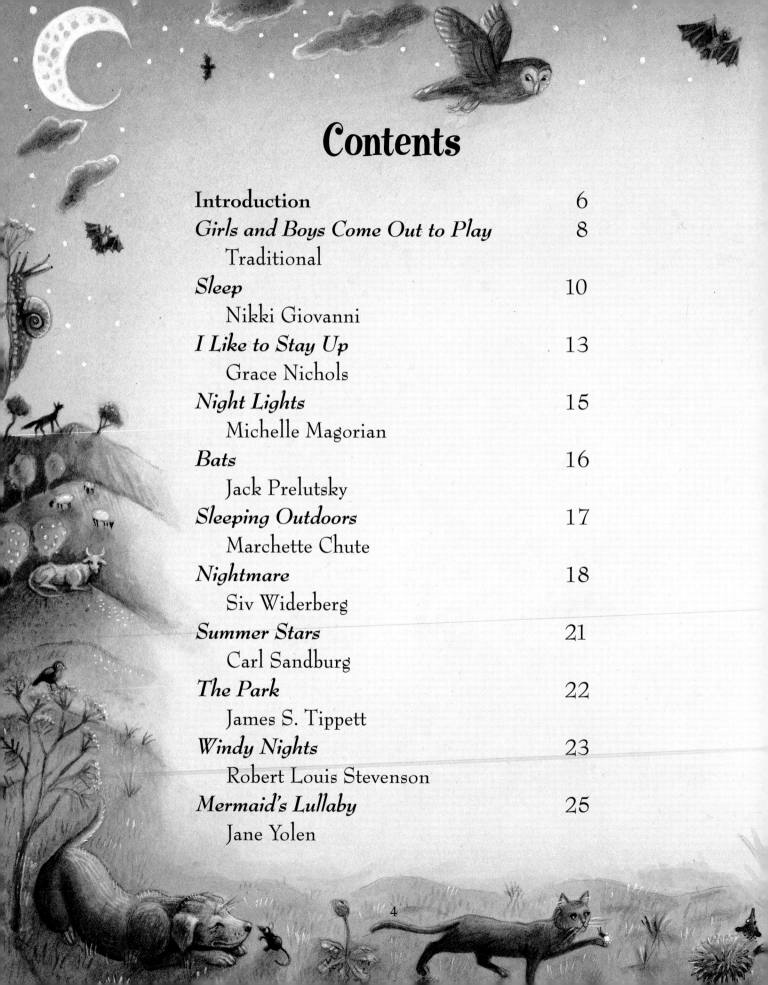

Contents

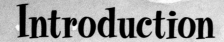

Introduction

Imagine yourself standing outside on a clear night. You are in the countryside, where neon streetlights don't spoil the darkness, looking at the sky and seeing the blackness filled with stars. Now imagine how it looks to a child. The stars hang in glittering patches in the sky, so tiny they could fill your hands and yet so far away that they are out of reach. Carl Sandburg's poem *Summer Stars* describes this feeling, and in *Silver* by Walter de la Mare, the poet lulls us into a dreamlike state in the way the moon does when her light turns the world to silver.

This collection of poems explores the mysteries of the night. Children have mixed feelings about darkness, even when the stars are shining — noises are scary and strange creatures stalk the night. Darkness is at once fascinating and frightening. I have gathered together poems old and new, humorous and serious, perfect for reading at bedtime, reading aloud to groups of children or for reading alone.

At bedtime, children separate from their families into the world of sleep, and many a child will attempt to put off the moment of departure, trying to find excuses for staying up. In *Night*, Arnold Adoff celebrates that delightful moment when you snuggle your child up under the covers and tuck him in. The poem is written in short words scattered on the page, and seems to mirror the way the child's head settles into the pillow and the bedclothes fold around him. In *I Like to Stay Up*, Grace Nichols captures the feelings of the child reluctant to go to bed as she wants to listen in to grown-up ghostie stories but then is scared when she is alone.

Poetry has a great way of making fears manageable. Darkness can be scary; things feel different at night. Children will recognize that other people experience similar feelings in poems, which seem to echo their fears. It gives

6

them a chance to explore their own experiences. *Nightmare* by Siv Widerberg treats the "Scratch Man" who lurks in the bedroom in a humorous way, and *The Park* by James Tippett touches on the comfort from lights outdoors — like "dandelions on a hill." Robert Louis Stevenson takes us right into the frightening sounds of the night in his poem *Windy Nights*. After the goodnight kiss, in the drowsy half-world between sleeping and waking, *Sleep* by Nikki Giovanni takes us to the imaginary forest of dotted rhinos and stripy horses, and Irene Rawnsley reminds us of the ghost which hides under our bed!

Children love rhymes and rhythm. They play with rhymes, start recognizing how words rhyme while still very small, and love repetition. In *Cat in the Dark*, John Agard spits out cat words in short bursts until he reaches the end of his poem when he lingers on the eyes of the cat "staring at the night." Ogden Nash is in a more restful mood when he lulls the child with *Sweet Dreams*.

This collection of poems can provide a starting point for children to start writing poetry for themselves. Children learn to love poetry by listening to it read aloud, and then having a go themselves. I have worked with many classes of children using poems like those in this collection and, hopefully, inspiring a new generation of writers.

Children are creatures of habit. Every night I say to my seven-year-old, "Night, night, sleep tight, hope the bugs don't bite." If I dare to forget, even in his sleepy state he reminds me of our ritual — I hope that these poems are short enough to go back to time and time again and will become part of your bedtime ritual.

Nikki Siegen-Smith

Girls and Boys Come Out to Play

Girls and boys, come out to play;
The moon doth shine as bright as day.
Leave your supper and leave your sleep,
And join your playfellows in the street.

Come with a whoop and come with a call,
Come with a good will or not at all.
Up the ladder and down the wall,
A half-penny loaf will serve us all.

You find milk and I'll find flour,
And we'll have a pudding in half an hour.
Come, let us dance on the open green,
And she who holds longest shall be our queen.

Traditional

8

Sleep

it was dark but when i blinked
twice i could see all the way deep
into the forest
and the lion came at me
and i really took care of him (pooped him twice
in the nose)
then a big rhinoceros with purple dots
and bright pink eyes
and i flung him over my head and threw
him into his mother's lap (where he belongs
since i'm so badddd)
then this striped horse neighed
up on his hind feet
but i jumped high and bit his ear
and he ran away crying
also the big bird whose wings blotched
out the moonlight swooped down
on me and i tickled his feet
just before the talons sunk in
and he laughed and laughed and slapped me
on the back and went home
so it's easy to see when the rat climbed
into my bed how tired
i was and why i called
moooooooommmmmmmmmiiiiiiieeeeeeeeeeee

Nikki Giovanni

I Like to Stay Up

I like to stay up
and listen
when big people talking
jumbie stories

I does feel
so tingly and excited
inside me

But when my mother say
"Girl, time for bed"

Then is when
I does feel a dread

Then is when
I does jump into me bed

Then is when
I does cover up
from me feet to me head

Then is when
I does wish I didn't listen
to no stupid jumbie story

Then is when
I does wish I did read
me book instead

Grace Nichols

Jumbie is a Guyanese word for "ghost"

13

14

Night Lights

My bedroom's at the very top
And when I am in bed
The buses from the street outside
Throw lights above my head.

They glide along my ceiling,
Sometimes fast and sometimes slow,
And I think of all the people
In the bus that's passed below.

And when it's dark and I can't sleep
I lie back and pretend
That every light crossing my room
Is a secret night-time friend.

Michelle Magorian

15

Bats

Bats have shiny leather wings,
bats do many clever things,
bats doze upside-down by day,
bats come out at night to play.

Bats cavort in soaring cliques,
sounding ultrasonic shrieks,
acrobatic in the sky
bats catch every bug they spy.

Jack Prelutsky

Sleeping Outdoors

Under the dark
is a star,
Under the star
is a tree,
Under the tree
is a blanket,
And under the
blanket is me.

Marchette Chute

17

Nightmare

I never say his name aloud
and don't tell anybody
I always close all the drawers
and look behind the door before I go to bed
I cross my toes and count to eight
and turn the pillow over three times
Still he comes sometimes
one two three
like a shot
glaring at me with his eyes,
grating with his nails
and sneering his big sneer —
the Scratch Man

Oh-oh, now I said his name!
Mama, I can't sleep!

Siv Widerberg

18

Summer Stars

Bend low again, night of summer stars.
So near, a long-arm man can pick off stars,
Pick off what he wants in the sky bowl,
So near you are, summer stars,
So near, strumming, strumming,
So lazy and hum-strumming.

Carl Sandburg

21

The Park

I'm glad that I
    Live near a park
For in the winter
    After dark
The park lights shine
    As bright and still
As dandelions
    On a hill.

James S. Tippett

22

Windy Nights

Whenever the moon and stars are set,
    Whenever the wind is high,
All night long in the dark and wet,
    A man goes riding by.
Late in the night when the fires are out,
Why does he gallop and gallop about?

Whenever the trees are crying aloud,
    And ships are tossed at sea,
By, on the highway, low and loud,
    By at the gallop goes he.
By at the gallop he goes, and then
By he comes back at the gallop again.

Robert Louis Stevenson

Mermaid's Lullaby

Hush, foam mocker,
Sleep, wave maker,
Close your eyes and dream,
Tide breaker.

Waves will rock you,
Whales will sing you,
Starfish a night-light
Will bring you.

Hush, deep diver,
Shush, shell keeper,
Be your finny mother's
Sleeper.

Jane Yolen

Sweet Dreams

I wonder as into bed I creep
What it feels like to fall asleep.
I've told myself stories, I've counted sheep
But I'm always asleep when I fall asleep.
Tonight my eyes I will open keep,
And I'll stay awake till I fall asleep,
Then I'll know what it feels like to fall asleep,
Asleep,
Asleeep,
Asleeeep...

Ogden Nash

House Ghosts

Airing cupboard ghosts
hold music practices
inside the water tank.

Television ghosts
poke crooked fingers
across your favorite program.

Chimney ghosts
sing one-note songs
over and over in owly voices.

Vacuum-cleaner ghosts
roar and the dust obeys them,
into the bag.

But the worst ghost
hides under your bed at night.

He makes no noise at all.

Irene Rawnsley

Cat in the Dark

Look at that!
Look at that!

But when you look
there's no cat.

Without a purr
just a flash of fur
and gone
like a ghost.

The most
you see
are two tiny
green traffic lights
staring at the night.

John Agard

29

Night Comes

Night comes
leaking
out of the sky.

Stars come
peeking.

Moon comes
sneaking
silvery-sly.

Who is
shaking,
shivery,
quaking?

Who is afraid
of the night?

Not I.

**Beatrice Schenk
de Regniers**

30

Silver

Slowly, silently, now the moon
Walks the night in her silver shoon;
This way, and that, she peers, and sees
Silver fruit upon silver trees;
One by one the casements catch
Her beams beneath the silvery thatch;
Couched in his kennel, like a log,
With paws of silver sleeps the dog;
From their shadowy cote the white breasts peep
Of doves in a silver-feathered sleep;
A harvest mouse goes scampering by,
With silver claws, and silver eye;
And moveless fish in the water gleam,
By silver reeds in a silver stream.

Walter de la Mare

31

Dipa

(A Song for Divali)

Light the lamp now.
Make bright
the falling night
wrapped in the leaves
of autumn.

Gone is the day.
Kindle the flame
to burn
in the dark.
Let it show
the way.

Lit is the lamp
of the moon.
Brilliant the stars.
Make them shine.
Let them unite.
Let there be light.

Ann Bonner

32

Cushlamochree

Cushlamochree, O Cushlamochree,
Shall you dance for the stars?
Shall you play with the sea?
Shall you swim like the whale?
Shall you follow the sun?
O Cushlamochree, has your dreaming begun?

Cariad Bach, O Cariad Bach,
Shall you sing to the moon?
Shall you shout for the dark?
Shall you whisper with bears?
Shall you waken the night?
O Cariad Bach, soft dreams and sleep tight.

Lucy Coats

Cushlamochree is Gaelic for "darling"
Cariad Bach is Welsh for "little darling"

35

Fireflies

If
You collect
Enough fireflies
You could
Read secrets
Under your blanket
All night long

Zaro Weil

36

Night

up
    to bed   your head
    down on the pillow

up
    to chin   your covers
    warm and tight tuck in
                    tuck in
                    tuck in
kiss
me
good

Arnold Adoff

37

Night Song

Come Easter
come Whitsun
come summer
come snow —
the stars in
the night sky
they rise and
they go:
the moon on
her journey,
the earth in
her flight,
they soothe us,
and shake us
from darkness
to light.

They calm us
and wake us,
they keep us,
and take us
from darkness —
from darkness
to light.....

Jean Kenward

Acknowledgments

Poems with attributed authors are listed in order of appearance; other entries are anonymous:

"Sleep" by Nikki Giovanni; "I Like to Stay Up" by Grace Nichols, reproduced with permission of Curtis Brown Ltd., London, on behalf of Grace Nichols. Copyright © Grace Nichols 1988; "Night Lights," from *Waiting For My Shorts To Dry* (p. 11, 12 lines) by Michelle Magorian, Viking Kestrel, 1989. Copyright © Michelle Magorian, 1989; "Bats," from *Something Big Has Been Here* by Jack Prelutsky, copyright © 1990 by Jack Prelutsky, reproduced by permission of Greenwillow Books, a division of William Morrow & Company, Inc., and William Heinemann (a division of Egmont Children's Books Limited); "Sleeping Outdoors" by Marchette Chute; "Nightmare" by Siv Widerberg, reprinted by permission of The Feminist Press at The City University of New York, from *I'm Like Me* by Siv Widerberg. Translated from the Swedish by Verne Moberg. Copyright © 1968, 1969, 1970, 1971 by Siv Widerberg. Translation copyright © 1973 by Verne Moberg; "Summer Stars," from *Smoke and Steel* by Carl Sandburg, copyright © 1920 by Harcourt Brace & Company and renewed 1948 by Carl Sandburg, reprinted by permission of the publisher; "The Park" by James S. Tippett; "Windy Nights" by Robert Louis Stevenson; "Mermaid's Lullaby" by Jane Yolen; "Sweet Dreams," from *Verses from 1929* by Ogden Nash. Copyright © 1961, 1962 by Ogden Nash. By permission of Little, Brown and Company; "House Ghosts," from *Dog's Dinner* by Irene Rawnsley, published by Methuen Children's Books (a division of Egmont Children's Books Limited); "Cat in the Dark," from *I Din Do Nuttin* by John Agard, reproduced by kind permission of The Bodley Head, London; "Night Comes" by Beatrice Schenk de Regniers; "Silver" by Walter de la Mare, from *The Complete Poems of Walter de la Mare*, reproduced by kind permission of the Literary Trustees of Walter de la Mare, and the Society of Authors as their representative; "Dipa" by Ann Bonner, copyright © 1989, first published in *Let's Celebrate*, Oxford University Press, compiled by John Foster in that year; "Cushlamochree," from *First Rhymes* by Lucy Coats, first published in the U. K. in 1994 by Orchard Books, a division of the Watts Publishing Group, 96 Leonard Street, London, EC2A 4RH; "Fireflies," from *Mud, Moon and Me* by Zaro Weil, first published in the U. K. in 1989 by Orchard Books, a division of the Watts Publishing Group, 96 Leonard Street, London, EC2A 4RH; "Night" by Arnold Adoff; "Night Song" by Jean Kenward, reproduced by kind permission of Jean Kenward.

The publishers have made every effort to contact holders of copyright material. If you have not received our correspondence, please contact us for inclusion in future editions.

BAREFOOT BOOKS publishes high-quality picture books for
children of all ages and specializes in the work of artists and writers from
many cultures. If you have enjoyed this book and would like to receive a copy of
our current catalog, please contact our New York office —
Barefoot Books Inc., 37 West 17th Street, 4th Floor East, New York, New York, 10010
e-mail: ussales@barefoot-books.com   website: www.barefoot-books.com